Learn to Read Armenian in 5 Days

ALEX HAKOBYAN

Happy Birthday, Alli!!!
    It is such a pleasure to work
with you and I am so thankful to
be working with you. [Sorry, that
wasn't so great.] You are a breath
of sunshine and I hope you
have a blessed year! Emily

ISBN-13: 978-0-9959305-5-1

CONTENTS

INTRODUCTION

Learning a new alphabet can be very intimidating for an English speaker only used to reading the Latin alphabet. This is partly why English speakers tend to stick to learning other languages that use the same alphabet, such as French, Spanish and Italian – because they seem a lot easier!

But learning a new alphabet does not have to be so difficult. The difficulty is finding a good system to learn the new alphabet so that the student does not get discouraged and give up before making any real progress. Making progress in the language is the best motivator.

The secret to learning a new alphabet is to be taught each letter separately, and then to practice how the new letters combine with letters you already know to read real words in the language in a structured way. This is not revolutionary – it is probably how you learned to read English – but it is not easy to find for other languages.

This book will teach you how to read the Armenian alphabet in exactly that way, and with this method you will be able to read Armenian in only 5 days or less! After that you will be able to enjoy the Armenian language and culture in a way that you were never able to before

THE ARMENIAN ALPHABET
Հայոց այբուբեն

The Armenian alphabet contains 39 letters and is written from left to right. The alphabet was introduced around 405 AD by Mesrop Mashtots, an Armenian linguist and ecclesiastical leader. The Armenian alphabet is graphically unique – it does not closely resemble any other alphabet – but there are some noticeable similarities with the Greek alphabet. It is only used to write the Armenian language.

Although it does not resemble the Latin alphabet used to write English (and other European languages) it is not a difficult alphabet to learn to read. This is because, with very few exceptions, letters are pronounced as they are written and written as they are pronounced, unlike languages such as English that make use of a lot of silent letters and historical spellings.

Like the Latin alphabet used to write English, the Armenian alphabet has both upper- and lowercase letters. Uppercase letters are used at the beginning of a sentence and in proper nouns.

There are, however, two different standard versions of the Armenian language, Eastern Armenian and Western Armenian. Eastern Armenian is the official and most widely spoken language in the Republic of Armenia, as well as the Armenian communities in Iran and Russia. Western Armenian was originally spoken in modern day Turkey during the Ottoman Empire, but is now almost exclusively spoken by Armenians in the diaspora and is classified as an endangered language.

This course uses the standard pronunciation and spelling of Eastern Armenian. The differences between Eastern and Western Armenian are largely a matter of accent and regular pronunciation changes; the alphabet is identical. For those interested in Western Armenian, see the section of this book titled "Differences Between Eastern and Western Armenian".

HOW TO USE THIS COURSE

The primary goal of this course book is to teach the reader to recognize the Armenian alphabet and to begin to read the Armenian language.

The main way this is accomplished is by teaching the individual pronunciations of each letter, and then utilizing "Practice" sections where the student can practice reading real Armenian words. These "Practice" sections are very important and the main way the student will start to feel comfortable with the Armenian alphabet. The answers to all "Practice" questions are included directly below the questions, but try to avoid looking at the answers until you have attempted to answer the questions yourself.

Throughout the book, the reader will also learn approximately 150 real Armenian words. These words have been carefully selected to be of maximum benefit to beginner students of the language and are a great starting point for students who want to continue their study of Armenian. In the end of the book there are two glossaries – one in thematic order and one in alphabetical order – where the student can study and memorize all the words learned in this course.

The course material has been designed to be completed slowly over five days, while reviewing lessons as necessary. You are encouraged to go at whatever pace you feel comfortable with and to feel free to go back to lessons to review as much as needed.

Good luck and I hope you enjoy the first step on your journey to learning the Armenian language.

UNIT 1 - ա, պ, մ, ն

The first letter introduced in this course is the Armenian letter ա. The pronunciation of this letter resembles the "a" sound in the English words "spa" and "father" (IPA: /ɑ/). The letter ա in its lowercase form resembles a handwritten English "w". The uppercase form is Ա.

The letter պ is pronounced like the English "p" in "pear" and "Peter" (IPA: /p/). Notice that this letter resembles ա but with a longer tail that continues below the line. The uppercase form is Պ.

Try to read the Armenian word below:

պապա

It is of course "papa", which means the same as papa or daddy in English.

The letter մ is pronounced like the English "m" in "mother" or "Mary" (IPA: /m/). This letter resembles a handwritten "u" with a hook on the top right side. The uppercase form is Մ.

Try to read the Armenian word below:

մամա

This is the Armenian word "mama", which means the same as mama or mommy in English.

The last letter of this unit is the letter ն. It is pronounced like the English "n" in "now" or "Nancy" (IPA: /n/). The letter ն resembles the letter մ, but with the hook on the left side of the "u" instead of the right side. The uppercase form is Ն.

PRACTICE

Try to recognize these English words in their Armenian disguises. The answers are below.
1. պան
2. մապ
3. նապ
4. ման
5. նանա

ANSWERS

1. pan
2. map
3. nap
4. man
5. Nana

UNIT 2 - ħ, ʮ, ʊn, u

The letter ħ is pronounced like the "ee" in "tree", or the "i" in "spaghetti" (IPA: /i/). It will be represented by "i" in this book. The letter ħ resembles the English letter "h" with the left side continuing below the line. The uppercase form is Ⱶ.

The letter ʮ is pronounced like the "k" sound in "keep" or "Kim" (IPA: /k/). The letter ʮ looks almost like a handwritten "4" or the letter ħ turned upside down. The uppercase form is Ӌ.

The letter ʊn is pronounced like the "t" sound in "tin" or "Tim" (IPA: /t/). The letter ʊn resembles a "u" and an "n" stuck together. The uppercase form is S, which resembles an uppercase "S" in English.

The letter u is pronounced like the "s" sound in "some" or "Sam" (IPA: /s/). The letter u resembles the English letter "u". The uppercase form is U.

TRY NOT TO CONFUSE

The letters u, ủ, and ꭒ are easily confused. Practice differentiating between u, which sounds like "s", ủ which sounds like "n" and ꭒ which sounds like "m".

PRACTICE

Try to recognize these English words in their Armenian disguises. Focus on the correct pronunciation and not necessarily the English spelling. The answers are below.

1. սի
2. տի
3. մի
4. կիպ
5. տիմ
6. պիկ
7.ստիմ
8. կամպ
9. սկամ
10. ստամպ

ANSWERS

1. see
2. tea
3. me
4. keep
5. team
6. peek
7. steam
8. camp
9. scam
10. stamp

UNIT 3 - o, ն, բ, գ, ռ

The Armenian letter o is pronounced like the "o" sound in "hope" or "rope" (IPA: /o/). The letter o usually is used at the beginning of a word in Armenian. The Armenian letter o looks and sounds just like the "o" in the English alphabet. The uppercase form is O.

In the middle or the end of a word, the same "o" sound is spelled with the letter ն instead of o. The letter ն resembles the letter "n" in English.

When ն is used at the beginning of a word instead of at the middle or end, it is pronounced "vo" instead of "o", i.e. with a "v" sound and an "o" sound. The uppercase form of this letter is Ո.

The letter բ is pronounced like the "b" sound in "bear" or "boss" (IPA: /b/). The uppercase form is Բ.

The letter գ is pronounced like the "g" sound in "good" or "Gary" (IPA: /g/). This letter resembles the letter "q" in English but with a small dash on the right hand side. The uppercase form is Գ.

The letter ռ is pronounced like the "r" sound in "red" or "robin" (IPA: /ɹ/). The lowercase letter sort of resembles an English "r" but stretched downwards. The uppercase form is Ռ.

TRY NOT TO CONFUSE

The letters հ, ռ, and բ can be easy to confuse as they look similar. Try to pay particular attention to these three letters until you are

5

comfortable with them. The letter ի sounds like "i" ("ee"), the letter ր sounds like "r" and the letter բ sounds liked "b".

PRACTICE

Try to read these real Armenian words. The English translation is given next to each word. The correct pronunciations are given in the answers below.

1. բանկ   (bank)
2. կին   (woman)
3. սիրտ   (heart)
4. ոսկոր   (bone)
5. գինի   (wine)
6. միս   (meat)
7. պանիր   (cheese)
8. կարմիր   (red)
9. սպիտակ   (white)
10. կրակ   (fire)

ANSWERS

1. bank
2. kin
3. sirt
4. voskor
5. gini
6. mis
7. panir
8. karmir
9. spitak
10. krak

UNIT 4 - Է, Ե, ʼn, վ, q

The Armenian letter Է is pronounced like the "e" sound in "bet" or "get" (IPA: /ɛ/). It will be represented as an "e" throughout this book, but remember not to pronounce it like "ee". This letter is usually used to make the "e" sound at the beginning of a word. The uppercase form is Է.

In the middle or end of a word, the same "e" sound is usually represented by the letter ե which looks very similar to Է but with the right side tip looped up at the end.

When the letter ե is used at the beginning of a word, however, it is pronounced "ye", i.e. a "y" sound followed by the "e" sound (IPA: /jɛ/). The uppercase form is Ե.

The letter ʼn is pronounced like the "d" sound in "den" or "David" (IPA: /d/). The uppercase form is Դ.

The letter վ is pronounced like the "v" sound in "very" (IPA: /v/). The uppercase form is Վ.

The letter q is pronounced like the "z" in "zoo" or "zebra" (IPA: /z/). The uppercase form is Զ.

TRY NOT TO CONFUSE

The letters Է and ե look very similar and it is easy to confuse them. In the middle or end of a word they are both pronounced "e" so this does not cause a problem, but at the beginning of a word, Է is pronounced "e" and ե is pronounced "ye" so it is important to distinguish between these two letters.

Our new letter վ, which is pronounced "v", looks similar to the letter կ from Unit 2, which is pronounced "k". Pay close attention to the "arms" of these two letters to differentiate between them.

The letter զ from this unit, which is pronounced "z", looks very similar to the letter գ which is pronounced "g". The main difference is the little tick on the right side of the letter զ.

PRACTICE

Try to read these Armenian words. The English translation is given next to each word. The correct pronunciations are given in the answers below.

1. կով   (cow)
2. երկիր   (country / state)
3. մարդ   (man)
4. գետ   (river)
5. վատ   (bad)
6. մեկ   (one)
7. մազ   (hair)
8. որդի   (son)

ANSWERS

1. kov
2. yerkir
3. mard
4. get
5. vat
6. mek
7. maz
8. vordi

UNIT 5 - ու, յ, ժ, շ, հ

Although written with two graphs, the combination ու is considered a single letter in Modern Armenian. It is pronounced like the "oo" in "boot" or the end of the word "shoe" (IPA: /u/).It will be represented by a "u" in this book.

The letter յ is pronounced like the "y" sound in "yes" or "yellow" at the beginning of a word. After another vowel it is pronounced like the "y" sound in "boy" or "bay", i.e. a glide that make a rising diphthong out of the preceding vowel (IPA: /j/). It will be represented by a "y" in this book. The uppercase form is Յ.

The letter ժ is pronounced like the "s" sound in "pleasure" or "measure" (IPA: /ʒ/). It will be represented as ž in this book. The uppercase form is Ժ.

The letter շ is pronounced like the "sh" sound in "she" or "shell" (IPA: /ʃ/). Note that even though this is two letters in English it actually represents a single sound and is a single letter in Armenian. It will be represented as š in this book. The uppercase form is Շ.

The letter հ is pronounced like the "h" sound in "happy" or "house" (IPA: /h/). Note that by a happy coincidence the lowercase form of this letter looks and is pronounced the same as in English. Note however that, unlike English, this letter is always pronounced, even in the middle or the end of a word. The uppercase form is Հ.

9

PRACTICE

Try to read these Armenian words. The English translation is given next to each word. The correct pronunciations are given in the answers below.

1. շուն (dog)
2. կատու (cat)
3. մուկ (mouse)
4. մայր (mother)
5. այգի (park / garden)
6. դուստր (daughter)
7. այո (yes)
8. հունիս (June)
9. ժամ (hour)
10. հայր (father)
11. արյուն (blood)
12. էժան (cheap)
13. տուն (house)
14. շուկա (market)

ANSWERS

1. šun
2. katu
3. muk
4. mayr
5. aygi
6. dustr
7. ayo
8. hunis
9. žam
10. hayr
11. aryun
12. ežan
13. tun
14. šuka

UNIT 6 - ը, լ, խ, ծ, ճ

The letter ը is pronounced like the "uh" sound at the end of the English words "sofa" or "salsa" when spoken in a normal, relaxed way (IPA: /ə/). This sound is pronounced a lot in English but it does not have its own letter in the English alphabet. In linguistics this sound is called a schwa. It will be represented by ə in this book. In contrast with other vowels, sometimes ը is not written but it is still pronounced. This is often the case between two or more consonants that would be difficult to pronounce without the ə sound in between. The uppercase form is Ը.

The letter լ is pronounced like the "l" sound in "little" or "less" (IPA: /l/). This letter is easy to remember as it does resemble the English "l". The uppercase form is Լ.

The letter խ is pronounced like the "ch" in the Scottish "loch", or the "ch" in the German "doch" or the "j" in the Spanish "ojos" (IPA: /x/). Although not a part of the English language it is not difficult to pronounce. It is really just a hard "h" sound with a bit of throat clearing. It will be represented by "x" in this book, but remember it is not pronounced "ks" like it English. The uppercase form is Խ.

The letter ծ is pronounced like the "ts" sound in "cats" or "its" (IPA: /ts/). Unlike English, in Armenian this sound can also be pronounced at the beginning of a word. It will be represented by "ts" in this book. The uppercase form is Ծ.

The letter ճ is pronounced like the "ch" in "church" or "cheese" (IPA: /tʃ/). Note that even though this sound is spelled with two letters in English, it is actually one sound and is spelled with a

11

single letter in Armenian. It will be represented by č in this book. The uppercase form is Ճ.

PRACTICE

Try to read these Armenian words. The English translation is given next to each word. The correct pronunciations are given in the answers below.

1. խոզ (pig)
2. ընկեր (friend)
3. սուրճ (coffee)
4. գլխարկ (hat)
5. ինը (nine)
6. լիճ (lake)
7. հեծանիվ (bicycle)
8. ծով (sea)
9. ապրիլ (April)
10. հուլիս (July)
11. երեխա (child)
12. մեծ (big)

ANSWERS

1. xoz
2. ənker
3. surč
4. gelxark
5. inə
6. lič
7. hetsaniv
8. tsov
9. april
10. hulis
11. yerexa
12. mets

UNIT 7 - ջ, ձ, թ, փ, ք

The letter ջ is pronounced like the "j" sound in "jump" or "jam" (IPA: /dʒ/). It will be represented by the letter "j" in this book. The uppercase form is Ջ.

The letter ձ is pronounced like the "ds" sound in "suds" (IPA: /dz/). It is the voiced version of the letter ծ. Unlike in English, ձ can begin a word in Armenian. It will be represented as "dz" in this course. The uppercase form is Ձ.

The letter թ is a more aspirated version of տ, meaning it is pronounced with a heavier puff of air than տ (IPA /tʰ/). The difference is hard to differentiate for English speakers but it is something like the difference between the "t" sound in "ten" vs. "steak". Notice that in the word "ten" there is a more forceful puff of air. It will be represented as t ʻ in this course, i.e. a "t" followed by a single quotation mark. The uppercase form is Թ.

Similarly, the letter փ is a more aspirated version of պ, meaning a "p" sound pronounced with more of a puff of air from your lips (IPA: /pʰ/). It will be represented as p ʻ in this course. The uppercase form is Փ.

The letter ք is a more aspirated version of կ (IPA: /kʰ/). It will be represented as k ʻ in this course. This Armenian letter resembles an English "p" that is underlined. The uppercase form is Ք.

TRY NOT TO CONFUSE

The letter Ձ is pronounced "j". Try not to confuse this new letter with the letter Շ from Unit 5, pronounced š. Pay close attention to the rounded loop at the top to distinguish these two letters.

The letter ձ is pronounced "dz". It looks very similar to ճ from Unit 6, which is pronounced č. In order to distinguish these two letters, pay close attention to the top of the letter.

PRACTICE

Try to read these Armenian words. The English translation is given next to each word. The correct pronunciations are given in the answers below.

1. ջուր   (water)
2. ականջ   (ear)
3. ձի   (horse)
4. ձուկ   (fish)
5. խնձոր   (apple)
6. խանութ   (store/shop)
7. քիթ   (nose)
8. փոքր   (small / little)
9. երեք   (three)
10. յոթ   (seven)
11. ութ   (eight)

ANSWERS

1. jur
2. akanj
3. dzi
4. dzuk
5. xəndzor (ə is not written)
6. xanutʿ
7. kʿitʿ
8. pʿokʿər (ə is not written)
9. yerekʿ
10. yotʿ
11. utʿ

UNIT 8 - ŋ, ꙅ, g

The letter ŋ is pronounced like the French or German "r" (IPA: /ʁ/). It is a sound that does not exist in English but if you know French or German you should be familiar with this sound, otherwise you may need to copy a native speaker in order to learn this sound. Following IPA, it will be represented as ʁ in this course. The uppercase form is Ꙍ.

The letter ꙅ is a more aspirated version of ᴪ, meaning it is pronounced like a "ch" sound but with a more pronounced puff of air (IPA: /tʃʰ/). In this course it will be represented by č'. The uppercase form is Ꙅ.

The letter g is a more aspirated version of ᴕ, meaning it is pronounced like a "ts" sound but with a more pronounced puff of air (IPA: /tsʰ/). In this course it will be represented by ts'. This lowercase form resembles an English "g". The uppercase form is Ꙃ.

TRY NOT TO CONFUSE

The new letter ŋ, which is pronounced "ʁ", looks a lot like ŋ from Unit 4, which is pronounced "d". The only difference is the little dash to the right of the letter ŋ.

17

PRACTICE

Try to read these Armenian words. The English translation is given next to each word. The correct pronunciations are given in the answers below.

1. եկեղեցի	(church)
2. սեղան	(table)
3. քաղաք	(city)
4. եղբայր	(brother)
5. տղա	(boy)
6. ոչ	(no)
7. աչք	(eye)
8. կանաչ	(green)
9. դեղին	(yellow)
10. գնացք	(train)
11. փողոց	(street)
12. դպրոց	(school)

ANSWERS

1. yekeʁetsʻi
2. seʁan
3. kʻaʁakʻ
4. yeʁbayr
5. təʁa
6. vočʻ
7. ačʻkʻ
8. kanačʻ
9. deʁin
10. gənatsʻkʻ (ə is not written)
11. pʻoʁotsʻ
12. dəprotsʻ (ə is not written)

18

UNIT 9 - եւ, ռ, ֆ

The letter եւ is spelled with two graphs but it is treated as a single letter in Modern Armenian. It is pronounced "ev" in the middle or the end of a word and "yev" when it is at the beginning of a word (IPA: /ɛv/ or /jɛv/). This letter is also sometimes written և, which is ligature of these symbols.

The letter ռ is a rolled "r", like the "r" in the Spanish word "rapido" or "rojo" (IPA: /r/). This takes some practice for an English speaker but it is not too difficult for most people. It will be represented as "rr" in this course, that is a double "r". The uppercase form is Ռ.

The letter ֆ is pronounced like the "f" sound in "fire" or "free" (IPA: /f/). Words with the letter ֆ are mostly foreign borrowings or onomatopoeic - very few genuine Armenian words have this letter or sound. The uppercase form is Ֆ.

PRACTICE

Try to read these Armenian words. The English translation is given next to each word. The correct pronunciations are given in the answers below.

1. սեւ   (black)
2. անձրեւ   (rain)
3. արեւ   (sun)
4. թռչուն   (bird)
5. ռեստորան   (restaurant)
6. աթոռ   (chair)
7. դուռ   (door)

19

8. ծառ	(tree)
9. ձեռք	(hand / arm)
10. սառույց	(ice)
11. սառն	(cold)
12. Ֆեյսբուք	(Facebook)
13. ֆիզիկոս	(physicist)

ANSWERS

1. sev
2. andzrev
3. arev
4. tʻərrčʻun
5. rrestoran
6. atʻorr
7. durr
8. tsar
9. dzerrkʻ
10. sarujtsʻ
11. sarrən (ə is not written)
12. feysbukʻ
13. fizikos

UNIT 10 - REVIEW

PRACTICE 1

Review the previous lessons by reading these real Armenian place names. The correct pronunciations are given in the Answers below.

1. Երևան
2. Արագած
3. Գյումրի
4. Վանաձոր
5. Շիրակ
6. Լոռի
7. Ախուրյան
8. Որոտան
9. Սևանա
10. Գեղարքունիք

ANSWERS 1

1. Yerevan
2. Aragats
3. Gyumri
4. Vanadzor
5. Širak
6. Lori
7. Axuryan
8. Vrotan
9. Sevana
10. Geʁarkʿunikʿ

PRACTICE 2

Review what you have learned in this book by reading the Armenian names below. The correct pronunciations are given in the Answers below.

1. Սարգսյան
2. Հակոբյան
3. Գրիգորյան
4. Քարտաշեան
5. Պետրոսյան
6. Աբրահամյան
7. Քոչարյան
8. Պետրոսյան

ANSWERS 2

1. Sargsyan
2. Hakobyan
3. Grigoryan
4. Kʻartašean
5. Petrosyan
6. Abrahamyan
7. Kʻočʻaryan
8. Petrosyan

ARMENIAN ALPHABET

Uppercase	Lowercase	Pronunciation
Ա	ա	[a]
Բ	բ	[b]
Գ	գ	[g]
Դ	դ	[d]
Ե	ե	[e], [ye]
Զ	զ	[z]
Է	է	[e]
Ը	ը	[ə]
Թ	թ	[tʻ]
Ժ	ժ	[ž]
Ի	ի	[i]
Լ	լ	[l]
Խ	խ	[x]
Ծ	ծ	[ts]
Կ	կ	[k]
Հ	h	[h]
Ձ	ձ	[dz]

Ղ	ղ	[ʁ]
Ճ	ճ	[č]
Մ	մ	[m]
Յ	յ	[y]
Ն	ն	[n]
Շ	շ	[š]
Ո	ո	[o], [vo]
Չ	չ	[čʻ]
Պ	պ	[p]
Ջ	ջ	[j]
Ռ	ռ	[rr]
Ս	ս	[s]
Վ	վ	[v]
Տ	տ	[t]
Ր	ր	[r]
Ց	ց	[tsʻ]
Ւ	ւ	[u]
Փ	փ	[pʻ]
Ք	ք	[kʻ]
	և	[yev], [ev]
Օ	o	[o]
Ֆ	ֆ	[f]

DIFFERENCES BETWEEN EASTERN AND WESTERN ARMENIAN

The table below shows the regular sound changes between Eastern and Western Armenian for anyone interested in the Western standard of the language.

Note that Eastern Armenian has a different sound for all letters, whereas Western Armenian pronounces several of the letters the same. Despite these pronunciation differences words are usually spelled the same in Eastern and Western Armenian with only some exceptions.

Armenian Letter	Eastern Armenian	Western Armenian
Բ	b	pʿ
պ	p	b
փ	pʿ	pʿ
գ	g	kʿ
կ	k	g
ք	kʿ	kʿ
դ	d	tʿ
տ	t	d
թ	tʿ	tʿ
ձ	dz	tsʿ

ð	ts	dz
g	ts ʿ	ts ʿ
ς	j	č ʿ
Ӄ	č	j
Ϛ	č ʿ	č ʿ
ք	r	r
ռ	rr	r

GLOSSARY – THEMATIC ORDER

ANIMALS

կենդանի	[kendani]	animal
շուն	[šun]	dog
կատու	[katu]	cat
ձուկ	[dzuk]	fish
թռչուն	[tʿərrčʿun]	bird
կով	[kov]	cow
խոզ	[xoz]	pig
մուկ	[muk]	mouse
ձի	[dzi]	horse

PEOPLE

անձ	[andz]	person
մայր	[mayr]	mother
մամա	[mama]	mommy / mama
հայր	[hayr]	father
պապա	[papa]	daddy / papa
որդի	[vordi]	son
դուստր	[dustr]	daughter
եղբայր	[yeʁbayr]	brother
քույր	[kʿuyr]	sister
ընկեր	[ənker]	friend
մարդ	[mard]	man
կին	[kin]	woman
տղա	[təʁa]	boy
աղջիկ	[aʁjik]	girl

երեխա	[yerexa]	child

TRANSPORTATION

գնացք	[gənats'k']	train
օդանավ	[odanav]	airplane
մեքենա	[mek'ena]	car
հեծանիվ	[hetsaniv]	bicycle
ավտոբուս	[avtobus]	bus
նավակ	[navak]	boat

LOCATION

քաղաք	[k'aʁak']	city
տուն	[tun]	house
փողոց	[p'oʁots']	street
օդանավակայան	[odanavakayan]	airport
հյուրանոց	[hyuranots']	hotel
ռեստորան	[rrestoran]	restaurant
դպրոց	[dəprots']	school
համալսարան	[hamalsaran]	university
այգի	[aygi]	park
խանութ	[xanut']	store / shop
հիվանդանոց	[hivandanots']	hospital
եկեղեցի	[yekeʁets'i]	church
երկիր	[yerkir]	country (state)
բանկ	[bank]	bank
շուկա	[šuka]	market

HOME

սեղան	[seʁan]	table
աթոռ	[atʿorr]	chair
պատուհան	[patuhan]	window
դուռ	[durr]	door
գիրք	[girkʿ]	book

CLOTHING

հագուստ	[hagust]	clothing
գլխարկ	[gəlxark]	hat
զգեստ	[əzgest]	dress
վերնաշապիկ	[vernašapik]	shirt
շալվար	[šalvar]	pants
կոշիկ	[košik]	shoe

BODY

մարմին	[marmin]	body
գլուխ	[glux]	head
երես	[yeres]	face
մազ	[maz]	hair
աչք	[ačʿkʿ]	eye
բերան	[beran]	mouth
քիթ	[kʿitʿ]	nose
ականջ	[akanj]	ear
ձեռք	[dzerrkʿ]	hand / arm
ոտք	[votkʿ]	foot / leg
սիրտ	[sirt]	heart

29

արյուն	[aryun]	blood
ոսկոր	[voskor]	bone
մորուք	[moruk']	beard

MISCELLANEOUS

այո	[ayo]	yes
ոչ	[voč']	no

FOOD & DRINK

սնունդ	[snund]	food
միս	[mis]	meat
հաց	[hats']	bread
պանիր	[panir]	cheese
խնձոր	[xəndzor]	apple
ջուր	[jur]	water
գարեջուր	[garejur]	beer
գինի	[gini]	wine
սուրճ	[surč]	coffee
թեյ	[t'ey]	tea
կաթ	[kat']	milk
նախաճաշ	[naxačaš]	breakfast
լանչ	[lanč']	lunch
ճաշ	[čaš]	dinner

COLORS

գույն	[guyn]	color
կարմիր	[karmir]	red
կապույտ	[kapuyt]	blue
կանաչ	[kanačʿ]	green
դեղին	[deʁin]	yellow
սեւ	[sev]	black
սպիտակ	[spitak]	white

NATURE

ծով	[tsov]	sea
գետ	[get]	river
լիճ	[lič]	lake
սար	[sar]	mountain
անձրեւ	[andzrev]	rain
ձյուն	[dzyun]	snow
ծառ	[tsarr]	tree
ծաղիկ	[tsaʁik]	flower
արեւ	[arev]	sun
լուսին	[lusin]	moon
քամի	[kʿami]	wind
երկինք	[yerkinkʿ]	sky
կրակ	[krak]	fire
սառույց	[sarujtsʿ]	ice

ADJECTIVES

մեծ	[mets]	big
փոքր	[p‘ok‘ər]	small
լավ	[lav]	good
վատ	[vat]	bad
տաք	[tak‘]	hot
սառն	[sarrən]	cold
էժան	[ežan]	cheap
թանկ	[t‘ank]	expensive
երջանիկ	[yerjanik]	happy
տխուր	[təxur]	sad

NUMBERS

մեկ	[mek]	one
երկու	[yerku]	two
երեք	[yerek‘]	three
չորս	[č‘ors]	four
հինգ	[hing]	five
վեց	[vets‘]	six
յոթ	[yot‘]	seven
ութ	[ut‘]	eight
ինը	[inə]	nine
տասը	[tasə]	ten

TIME

| օր | [or] | day |
| ամիս | [amis] | month |

տարի	[tari]	year
ժամ	[žam]	hour
այսոր	[aysor]	today
վաղը	[vaʁə]	tomorrow
երեկ	[yerek]	yesterday

DAYS OF THE WEEK

կիրակի	[kiraki]	Sunday
երկուշաբթի	[yerkušabtʻi]	Monday
երեքշաբթի	[yerekʻšabtʻi]	Tuesday
չորեքշաբթի	[čʻorekʻšabtʻi]	Wednesday
հինգշաբթի	[hingšabtʻi]	Thursday
ուրբաթ	[urbatʻ]	Friday
շաբաթ	[šabatʻ]	Saturday

MONTHS

հունվար	[hunvar]	January
փետրվար	[pʻetərvar]	February
մարտ	[mart]	March
ապրիլ	[april]	April
մայիս	[mayis]	May
հունիս	[hunis]	June
հուլիս	[hulis]	July
օգոստոս	[ogostos]	August
սեպտեմբեր	[september]	September
հոկտեմբեր	[hoktember]	October
նոյեմբեր	[noyember]	November
դեկտեմբեր	[dektember]	December

33

PROPER NAMES

հայ	[hay]	Armenian
Հայաստան	[hayastan]	Armenia
Երևան	[yerevan]	Yerevan

GLOSSARY – ALPHABETICAL ORDER

– Ա ա –

աթոռ	[atʿorr]	chair
ականջ	[akanj]	ear
աղջիկ	[aʁjik]	girl
ամիս	[amis]	month
այգի	[aygi]	park
այո	[ayo]	yes
այսոր	[aysor]	today
անձ	[andz]	person
անձրեւ	[andzrev]	rain
աչք	[ačʿkʿ]	eye
ապրիլ	[april]	April
ավտոբուս	[avtobus]	bus
արեւ	[arev]	sun
արյուն	[aryun]	blood

– Բ բ –

բանկ	[bank]	bank
բերան	[beran]	mouth

– Գ գ –

գարեջուր	[garejur]	beer
գետ	[get]	river

35

գինի	[gini]	wine
գիրք	[girkʿ]	book
գլխարկ	[gəlxark]	hat
գլուխ	[glux]	head
գնացք	[gənatsʿkʿ]	train
գույն	[guyn]	color

– Դ դ –

դեկտեմբեր	[dektember]	December
դեղին	[deʁin]	yellow
դուռ	[durr]	door
դուստր	[dustr]	daughter
դպրոց	[dəprotsʿ]	school

– Ե ե –

եկեղեցի	[yekeʁetsʿi]	church
եղբայր	[yeʁbayr]	brother
երեխա	[yerexa]	child
երեկ	[yerek]	yesterday
երես	[yeres	face
Երևան	[yerevan]	Yerevan
երեք	[yerekʿ]	three
երեքշաբթի	[yerekʿšabtʿi]	Tuesday
երկինք	[yerkinkʿ]	sky
երկիր	[yerkir]	country
երկու	[yerku]	two
երկուշաբթի	[yerkušabtʿi]	Monday
երջանիկ	[yerjanik]	happy

– Զ q –

զգեստ	[əzgest]	dress

– Է է –

էժան	[ežan]	cheap

– Ը ը –

ընկեր	[ənker]	friend

– Թ թ –

թանկ	[tʿank]	expensive
թեյ	[tʿey]	tea
թռչուն	[tʿərrčʿun]	bird

– Ժ ժ –

ժամ	[žam]	hour

– Ի ի –

ինը	[inə]	nine

– Լ լ –

լանչ	[lančʿ]	lunch
լավ	[lav]	good
լիճ	[lič]	lake
լուսին	[lusin]	moon

– Խ խ –

խանութ	[xanutʿ]	shop
խնձոր	[xəndzor]	apple
խոզ	[xoz]	pig

– Ծ ծ –

ծաղիկ	[tsaʁik]	flower
ծառ	[tsarr]	tree
ծով	[tsov]	sea

– Կ կ –

կաթ	[katʿ]	milk
կանաչ	[kanačʿ]	green
կապույտ	[kapuyt]	blue
կատու	[katu]	cat
կարմիր	[karmir]	red
կենդանի	[kendani]	animal
կին	[kin]	woman
կիրակի	[kiraki]	Sunday

կոշիկ	[košik]	shoe
կով	[kov]	cow
կրակ	[krak]	fire

– Հ h –

հագուստ	[hagust]	clothing
համալսարան	[hamalsaran]	university
հայ	[hay]	Armenian
Հայաստան	[Hayastan]	Armenia
հայր	[hayr]	father
հաց	[hatsʻ]	bread
հեծանիվ	[hetsaniv]	bicycle
հինգ	[hing]	five
հինգշաբթի	[hingšabtʻi]	Thursday
հիվանդանոց	[hivandanotsʻ]	hospital
հյուրանոց	[hyuranotsʻ]	hotel
հոկտեմբեր	[hoktember]	October
հուլիս	[hulis]	July
հունիս	[hunis]	June
հունվար	[hunvar]	January

– Ձ ծ –

ձեռք	[dzerrkʻ]	hand / arm
ձի	[dzi]	horse
ձյուն	[dzyun]	snow
ձուկ	[dzuk]	fish

39

– Ճ ճ –

Ճաշ	[čaš]	dinner

– Մ մ –

մազ	[maz]	hair
մամա	[mama]	mama
մայիս	[mayis]	May
մայր	[mayr]	mother
մարդ	[mard]	man
մարմին	[marmin]	body
մարտ	[mart]	March
մեծ	[mets]	big
մեկ	[mek]	one
մեքենա	[mekʿena]	car
միս	[mis]	meat
մորուք	[morukʿ]	beard
մուկ	[muk]	mouse

– Յ յ –

յոթ	[yotʿ]	seven

– Ն ն –

նախաճաշ	[naxačaš]	breakfast
նավակ	[navak]	boat
նոյեմբեր	[noyember]	November

– Շ 2 –

շաբաթ	[šabatʿ]	Saturday
շալվար	[šalvar]	pants
շուկա	[šuka]	market
շուն	[šun]	dog

– Ո n –

ոչ	[vočʿ]	no
ոսկոր	[voskor]	bone
ոտք	[votkʿ]	foot / leg
որդի	[vordi]	son

– ՈՒ nι –

ութ	[utʿ]	eight
ուրբաթ	[urbatʿ]	Friday

– Չ ᷉ –

չորեքշաբթի	[čʿorekʿšabtʿi]	Wednesday
չորս	[čʿors]	four

– Պ պ –

պանիր	[panir]	cheese
պապա	[papa]	papa

պատուհան	[patuhan]	window

– Ջ ջ –

ջուր	[jur]	water

– Ռ ռ –

ռեստորան	[rrestoran]	restaurant

– Ս ս –

սառն	[sarrən]	cold
սառույց	[sarujtsʿ]	ice
սար	[sar]	mountain
սեղան	[seʁan]	table
սեպտեմբեր	[September]	September
սեւ	[sev]	black
սիրտ	[sirt]	heart
սնունդ	[snund]	food
սուրճ	[surč]	coffee
սպիտակ	[spitak]	white

– Վ վ –

վաղը	[vaʁə]	tomorrow
վատ	[vat]	bad
վերնաշապիկ	[vernašapik]	shirt

| վեց | [vetsʿ] | six |

– S տ –

տասը	[tasə]	ten
տարի	[tari]	year
տաք	[takʿ]	hot
տխուր	[təxur]	sad
տղա	[təʁa]	boy
տուն	[tun]	house

– Ֆ ֆ –

ֆետրվար	[pʿetərvar]	February
փողոց	[pʿoʁotsʿ]	street
փոքր	[pʿokʿər]	small

– Ք ք –

քաղաք	[kʿaʁakʿ]	city
քամի	[kʿami]	wind
քիթ	[kʿit]	nose
քույր	[kʿuyr]	sister

– O o –

| oգոստոս | [ogostos] | August |
| oդանավ | [odanav] | airplane |

43

օդանավակայան	[odanavakayan]	airport
օր	[or]	day

– Ֆ ֆ –

Ֆեյսբուք	[Feysbukʿ]	Facebook
ֆիզիկոս	[fizikos]	physicist

Other language learning titles available from Wolfedale Press:

Learn to Read Arabic in 5 Days
Learn to Read Bulgarian in 5 Days
Learn to Read Georgian in 5 Days
Learn to Read Greek in 5 Days
Learn to Read Modern Hebrew in 5 Days
Learn to Read Persian (Farsi) in 5 Days
Learn to Read Russian in 5 Days
Learn to Read Ukrainian in 5 Days